First published 1997 © Robert Frederick Ltd.,
4 North Parade, Bath, BA1 1LF

Printed and bound in China

TO A SPECIAL

GRANDMOTHER

An English Country Cottage by James Matthews
City Hall Gallery, Chester, Fine Art Photograph Library

"We never know the love of our parents for us till we have become parents."
Henry Ward Beecher

"There is only one pretty child in the world, and every mother has it."
Chinese Proverb

"Any cook should be able to run the country."
Lenin

"Every baby born into the world is a finer one than the last."
Charles Dickens: Nicholas Nickleby

"Sometimes when one person is missing, the whole world seems depopulated."
Lamartine

"Weep not that the world changes – did it keep
A stable, changeless state, 'twere cause indeed to weep."
William Cullen Bryant

"There's no vocabulary
For love within a family, love that's lived in
But not looked at, love within the light of which
All else is seen, the love within which
All other love finds speech.
This love is silent."

T. S. Eliot

"Good nature is worth more than knowledge, more than money,
more than honour, to the persons who possess it."

Henry Ward Beecher

"It's not hard to make decisions when you know what your values are."

Roy Disney

"All love is sweet,
Given or returned. Common as light is love,
And its familiar voice wearies not ever."

Shelley

Villa at Rueil, 1882
by Edouard Manet

A Still Life of Peonies in a Vase
by Marguerite Carrier-Roy, B1870
Sotheby's Picture Library

"Loyalty brings its own reward."

Proverbs 11.17

"The ineffable joy of forgiving and being forgiven forms an ecstasy
that might well arouse the envy of the gods."

Elbert Hubbard

"Come to me in my dreams, and then,
By day I shall be well again,
For then the night will more than pay
The hopeless longing of the day."

Matthew Arnold

"If love lives on hope, it dies with it; it is a fire which goes out for want of fuel."

Pierre Corneille

"'Tis better to have loved and lost,
Than never to have loved at all."

Alfred Tennyson

"Monday's child is fair of face,
Tuesday's child is full of grace,
Wednesday's child is full of woe,
Thursday's child has far to go,
Friday's child is loving and giving,
Saturday's child works hard for a living,
But the child that's born on the Sabbath day
Is bonny and blithe and good and gay."

Anon

"Security is when I'm very much in love with somebody extraordinary
who loves me back."

Shelley Winters

"The most fortunate of men,
Be he a king or commoner, is he
Whose welfare is assured in his own home."

Johann Wolfgang von Goethe

Clematis in a Crystal Vase
by Edouard Manet

A Still Life of Grapes Resting on a Marble Ledge
by G. Van Spaendonck (1746-1822)
Rafael Valls Gallery, London/
Bridgeman Art Library, London

"Pride makes us do things well.
But it is love that makes us do them to perfection."
Author Unidentified

"There never was a child so lovely but his mother was glad to get him asleep."
Ralph Waldo Emerson

"Courtesy wins woman all as well
As valour may, but he that closes both
Is perfect."
Lord Tennyson

"We only part to meet again."
John Gay

"All changes, even the most longed for, have their melancholy;
for what we leave behind us is a part of ourselves;
we must die to one other life before we can enter into another!"
Anatole France

"Unity of feelings and affections makes the strongest relationship."

Publilius Syrus

"A man seldom thinks with more earnestness of anything
than he does of his dinner."

Samuel Johnson

"Through our own recovered innocence we discern the innocence
of our neighbours."

Thoreau

"Tears may linger at nightfall,
but joy comes in the morning."

Psalms 126:5

"The fruit of the Spirit is love, joy, peace, patience, kindness,
goodness, trustfulness, gentleness and self-control;
no law can touch such things as these."

Paul, 1st Century

A Picturesque Cottage Garden
by Arther Claude Strachan (1865-1954)
Anthony Mitchell Fine Paintings, Fine Art Photograph Library

Summer Landscape by Auguste Renoir

"Marriage is an empty box. It remains empty unless
you put in more than you take out."
Author Unidentified

"We were gentle among you, even as a nurse cherisheth her children."
1 Thessalonians 2:7

"Of cheerfulness, or a good temper –
the more it is spent, the more of it remains."
Ralph Waldo Emerson

"The gods help him who helps himself."
Euripides

"Behold how good and pleasant it is for brethren to dwell together in unity."
Psalms 133:1

"Laughter has no foreign accent."
Paul Lowney

"Men always want to be a woman's first love; women have a more subtle instinct: what they like is to be a man's last romance."
Author Unidentified

"There is no more lovely, friendly and charming relationship, communion or company than a good marriage."
Martin Luther

"Don't let what you cannot do interfere with what you can do."
John Wooden

"Good-humour is a philosophic state of mind; it seems to say to Nature that we take her no more seriously than she takes us."
Ernest Renan

"Love doesn't sit there like a stone, it has to be made, like bread; remade all the time, made new."
Ursula K. le Guin

Woman with
Chrysanthemums
by Edgar Degas

The Dancing Bear
by Frederick Morgan (1856-1927)
Roy Miles Gallery, 29 Bruton Street,
London/Bridgeman Art Library London

"She will never win him, whose
Words had shown she feared to lose."
Dorothy Parker

"I'd rather have roses on my table than diamonds on my neck."
Emma Goldman

"Nothing is so strong as gentleness, and nothing is so gentle as real strength."
Ralph W. Sockman

"The most wasted day is that in which we have not laughed."
Chamfort

"When thou prayest, rather let thy heart be without words
than thy words without heart."
John Bunyan

"'Tis an ill cook that cannot lick his own fingers."
Shakespeare: Romeo & Juliet

"There is never a wrong time to do the right thing."
Author Unidentified

"Children are the true connoisseurs.
What's precious to them has no price, only value."
Bel Kaufman

"Change is the law of life. And those who look only to the past or the present
are certain to miss the future."
John F. Kennedy

"It is innocence that is full and experience that is empty.
It is innocence that wins and experience that loses."
Charles Péguy

"What is uttered from the heart alone
Will win the hearts of others to your own."
Johann Wolfgang von Goethe

Poppies at Argenteuil by Claude Monet

A Wayside Cottage
by Helen Allingham (1848-1926)
Haynes Fine Art,
Fine Art Photograph Library

"One who knows how to show and to accept kindness
will be a friend better than any possession."

Sophocles

"To understand all is to pardon all."
[Tout comprendre rend très indulgent.]

Anna Louise de Stael

"It needs courage to let our children go, but we are trustees and stewards
and have to hand them back to life – to God. As the old saying puts it:
'What I gave I have.' We have to love them and lose them."

Alfred Torrie

"Generosity gives assistance rather than advice."

Vauvenargues

"Pray as if everything depended on God and act as if everything
depended on oneself."

St. Ignatius of Loyola

"You can accomplish by kindness what you cannot do by force."
Publilius Syrus

"A man's wife has more power over him that the state has."
Ralph Waldo Emerson

"I am only one; but still I am one. I cannot do everything, but still I can do something; I will not refuse to do something I can do."
Helen Keller

"He is poor indeed that can promise nothing."
Thomas Fuller

"Our hours in love have wings; in absence crutches."
Colley Cibber

"Plus ça change, plus c'est la même chose."
[The more things change, the more they remain the same.]
Alphonse Karr

A Still Life of Roses
by F. Fenetti
19th/20th Century
Sotheby's Picture
Library

Monet's Garden at Argenteuil (Dahlias), 1873, by Claude Monet

"I like the dreams of the future better than the history of the past."
Thomas Jefferson

"Gratitude is the most exquisite form of courtesy."
Jacques Maritain

"We come nearest to the great when we are great in humility."
Rabindranath Tagore

"Gratitude is the heart's memory."
French Proverb

"Ask, and you will receive; seek and you will find; knock,
and the door will be opened."
Matthew 11:24

"Only two things are necessary to keep one's wife happy. One is to let her think
she is having her own way, and the other, to let her have it."
Lyndon B. Johnson

"The art of dining well is no slight art, the pleasure not a slight pleasure."

Montaigne

"We are all wise for other people, none for himself."

Ralph Waldo Emerson

"Gratefulness is the poor man's payment."

English Proverb

"Better is it to be of a humble spirit with the lowly
than to divide the spoil with the proud."

Proverbs 16:19

"The quality of a person's life is in direct proportion to their commitment
to excellence, regardless of their chosen field of endeavour."

Vince Lombardi

"Always be a little kinder than necessary."

James M. Barrie

Blind Man's Bluff
by Frederick Morgan (1856-1927)
Roy Miles Gallery, 29 Bruton
Street, London/Bridgeman Art
Library, London

Garden of Les Mathurins at Pontoise by Camille Pissarro

"A friend is a person with whom I may be sincere.
Before him I may think aloud."

Ralph Waldo Emerson

"Strange to see how a good dinner and feasting reconciles everybody."

Samuel Pepys

"No one is so accursed by fate,
No one so utterly desolate,
But some heart, though unknown,
Responds unto his own."

H. W. Longfellow

"You will find as you look back upon your life that the moments when you have
really lived are the moments when you have done things in the spirit of love."

Henry Drummond

"Children are the anchors that hold a mother to life."

Sophocles

"Challenges can be stepping stones or stumbling blocks.
It's just a matter of how you view them."
Author Unidentified

"Real generosity is doing something nice for someone who'll never find it out."
Frank A. Clark

"Let the children come to me; do not try to stop them;
for the kingdom of Heaven belongs to such as these."
Matthew 19:14

"The man who wins may have been counted out several times,
but he didn't hear the referee."
H. E. Jansen

"The proper office of a friend is to side with you when you are in the wrong.
Nearly anybody will side with you when you are in the right."
Mark Twain

At Cocking, Sussex by James Matthews
Harper Fine Art, Fine Art Photograph Library

JAMES MATTHEWS.

Water Lilies. 1914
ny Claude Monet

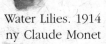

"Hospitality is to be shown even towards an enemy.
The tree doth not withdraw its shade, even from the woodcutter."
The Hitopadesa

"Love feeds on hope, they say, or love will die – Ah miserie!
Yet my love lives, although no hope have I! – Ah miserie!"
W. S. Gilbert

"Nothing flatters a man as much as the happiness of his wife;
he is always proud of himself as the source of it."
Samuel Johnson

"Married couples who love each other tell each other
a thousand things without talking."
Chinese Proverb

"In the confrontation between the stream and the rock,
the stream always wins – not through strength but by perseverance."
Author Unidentified

"Our life is what our thoughts make it."

Marcus Aurelius

"Aim at the sun, and you may not reach it; but your arrow will fly far higher than if aimed at an object on a level with yourself."

J. Hawes

"A kiss, when all is said, what is it?
An oath that's given closer than before;
A promise more precise; the sealing of
Confessions that till then were barely breathed;
A rosy dot placed on the *i* in loving."

Edmond Rostand

"For what is faith unless it is to believe what you do not see?"

St. Augustine

"When there is room in the heart there is room in the house."

Danish Proverb

Fruit Still Life
by Jan Van Huysum

Young Woman Bathing her
Feet 1895,
by Camille Pissarro

"Who never climbed high never fell low."
Thomas Fuller

"Cooking is like love. It should be entered into with abandon or not at all."
Harriet van Horne

"Your friend is the man who knows all about you and still likes you."
Elbert Hubbard

"To be without some of the things you want is an
indispensable part of happiness."
Bertrand Russell

"Often the difference between a successful marriage and a mediocre one
consists of leaving about three or four things a day unsaid."
Harlan Miller

"The smallest act of kindness is worth more than the grandest intention."
Author Unidentified

"The man who has never made a fool of himself in love
will never be wise in love."
Theodor Reik

"Great works are performed not by strength but by perseverance."
Samuel Johnson

"We find it hard to get and to keep any private property in thought.
Other people are all the time saying the same things we are
hoarding to say when we get ready."
Oliver Wendell Holmes Sr.

"The height of cleverness is to be able to conceal it."
François de la Rochefoucauld

"'Whoever receives one of these children in my name', he said 'receives me;
and whoever receives me, receives not me but the One who sent me'."
Mark 9.37

Roses on a Riverbank by
Madeleine Lemaire (1845-1928)
Sotheby's Picture Library

"When you have been wronged, a poor memory is your best response."
Author Unidentified

"We find delight in the beauty and happiness of children
that makes the heart too big for the body."
Ralph Waldo Emerson

"A pessimist is a man who thinks all women are bad.
An optimist is the one who hopes they are."
Chauncey Depew

"A man's home is his wife's castle."
Alexander Chase

"The need for devotion to something outside ourselves is even
more profound than the need for companionship.
If we are not to go to pieces or wither away, we all must have some
purpose in life; for no man can live for himself alone."
Ross Parmenter

"We never make sport of religion, politics, race or mothers.
A mother never gets hit with a custard pie. Mothers-in-law – yes.
But mothers – never."
Mack Sennett

"Happiness is not the absence of problems; but the ability to deal with them."
Author Unidentified

"There's nothing worth the wear of winning,
But laughter and the love of friends."
Hilaire Belloc

"Between our birth and death we may touch understanding
as a moth brushes a window with its wing."
Christopher Fry

"Marriage is popular because it combines the maximum of temptation
with the maximum of opportunity."
Shelley

The Swing, 1876
by Auguste Renoir

Springtime, by Claude Monet

"We should not let our fears hold us back from pursuing our hopes."
John F. Kennedy

"I expect to pass through life but once. If, therefore, there be any
kindness I can show, or any good thing I can do for any fellow being,
let me do it now, for I shall not pass this way again."
William Penn

"God could not be everywhere, so He made mothers."
Jewish Proverb

"Have patience with all things, but chiefly have patience with yourself.
Do not lose courage in considering your own imperfections, but instantly
set about remedying them – every day begin the task anew."
Ascribed to St. Francis de Sales

"There is not so much comfort in the having of children
as there is in the sorrow of parting with them."
Thomas Fuller

"When I was at home, I was in a better place."
Shakespeare: As You Like It

"The greatest wealth is to live content with little, for there is never want where the mind is satisfied."
Lucretius

"He who does not hope to win has already lost."
José Joaquin Olmedo

"To believe is to be strong. Doubt cramps energy. Belief is power."
Frederick William Robertson

"Children are poor men's riches."
English Proverb

"Immature love says: 'I love you because I need you.'
Mature love says: 'I need you because I love you.' "
Erich Fromm

The Luncheon
by Claude Monet

A Meeting on the Bridge by Emile Claus (1849-1924)
Sotheby's Picture Library

"There are two sorts of constancy in love; the one comes from
the constant discovery in our beloved of new grounds for love,
and the other comes from making it a point of honour to be constant."

François de la Rochefoucauld

"Success is getting what you want. Happiness is liking what you get."

Author Unidentified

"To be patient shows great understanding;
quick temper is the height of folly."

Proverbs 14:29

"If it were not for hopes, the heart would break."

Thomas Fuller

"I keep my friends as misers do their treasure, because, of all the things
granted us by wisdom, none is greater or better than friendship."

Pietro Aretino

"Modesty gives the maid greater beauty than even the bloom of youth, it bestows on the wife the dignity of a matron, and reinstates the widow in her virginity."
Joseph Addison

"The magic of first love is our ignorance that it can ever end."
Benjamin Disraeli

"There is no slave out of heaven like a loving women; and, of all loving women, there is no such slave as a mother."
Henry Ward Beecher

"We have no more right to consume happiness without producing it than to consume wealth without producing it."
George Bernard Shaw

"A woman only obliges a man to secrecy that she may have the pleasure of telling herself."
William Congreve

The Garden Path
by James Matthews
City Hall Gallery, Chester,
Fine Art Photograph Library

A Still Life of Roses in a Vase
by Paul Biva (1851-1900)
Sotheby's Picture Library

"Content makes poor men rich; discontent makes rich men poor."
Benjamin Franklin

"Only the person who has faith in himself is able to be faithful to others."
Erich Fromm

"Grief can take care of itself, but to get the full value of joy
you must have somebody to divide it with."
Mark Twain

"Honesty is the first chapter in the book of wisdom."
Thomas Jefferson

"A kiss can be a comma, a question mark or an exclamation point.
That's basic spelling that every woman ought to know."
Mistinguett

"Love is an act of endless forgiveness, a tender look which becomes a habit."
Peter Ustinov

"Mother is the name for God in the lips and hearts of little children."

W. M. Thackeray

"There is nothing like staying at home for real comfort."

Jane Austen

"The love we give away is the only love we keep."

Elbert Hubbard

"Where parents do too much for their children, the children will not do much for themselves."

Elbert Hubbard

"Womanliness means only motherhood;
All love begins and ends there."

Robert Browning

"What value has compassion that does not take its object in its arms?"

Saint-Exupéry

The Artist's Garden, Irises
by Claude Monet

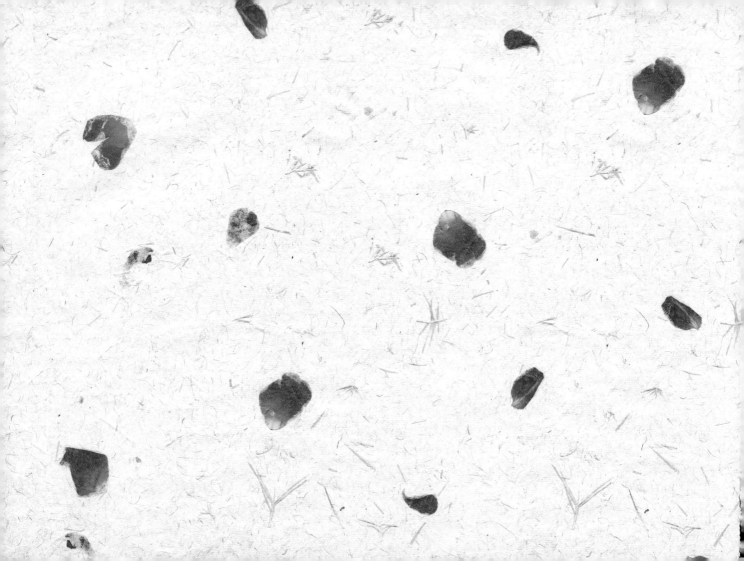